COCKTAILS
Hilary Walden

Cocktails was first published in 1983 by
Octopus Books Limited
59 Grosvenor Street, London W1

This new revised edition first published in 1985
© 1985 Hennerwood Publications Limited

Some of the recipes were first published in 1982 by
Octopus Books Limited in *Cocktails, Punches & Cups*

ISBN 0 86273 220 4

Produced by Mandarin Publishers Ltd
22a Westlands Road, Quarry Bay, Hong Kong

Printed in Hong Kong

CONTENTS

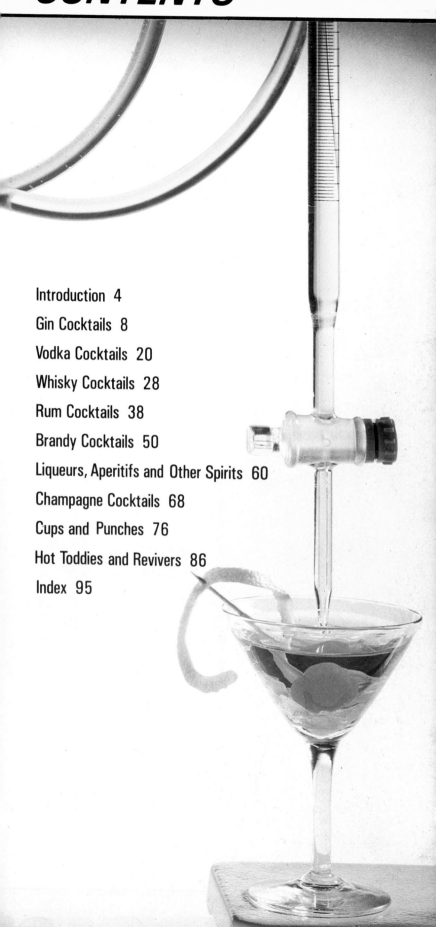

INTRODUCTION

To a professional barman a cocktail is a short drink of about 85–120 ml/3–4 fl oz, and anything longer would be referred to as a long drink or a mixed drink. Mixed drinks, both hot and cold, have been around for hundreds of years but cocktails as we know them are only comparatively recent inventions. Just when, and how, they first came into existence is a subject of some conjecture, and there are several, all rather lengthy, versions. What is certain, however, is that the drinks which are currently experiencing a new lease of life, had their true beginnings in the Prohibition Era in the U.S.A. Originally they were designed to create something drinkable from an assortment of poorly made, inferior liquors, but the idea was soon seized upon by those who had access to good quality liquor. When the ban was lifted in 1933 and the overall standards of liquor were raised, many of the more acceptable concoctions were refined, more created, and the cocktail boom really began. The idea of cocktails appealed to other nations and they travelled far and wide, including to England. Here, the cocktail hour, between 5.30 and 7.30, fitted nicely into the gap left by the decline in afternoon tea, providing a most pleasant way of socializing, particularly for the younger 'chic' set, whiling the time away until dinner. The Second World War effectively stilled the cocktail shakers and they were not to be taken up again in this country to any extent until the late 1970s, early 1980s. Today, they are probably even more popular than they were. There is a greater range of spirits to choose from and many new liqueurs have made an appearance, but, more significantly, today's cocktail drinkers come from a much broader spectrum of the population.

Making Cocktails

Making cocktails and other mixed drinks is like making anything else—the various components can be thrown together in a haphazard way, or they can be carefully assembled. Which method is used is usually reflected in the final product.

The making of cocktails is not difficult but will be even easier, and more successful, if a few simple 'ground rules' are observed:

● Prepare on a surface that will not be spoilt if marked by bottles, glasses or drips and which can be wiped down easily
● Keep all drinks in a cool place. Preferably keep all 'mixers' and fruit juices in a refrigerator
● Always add ice to a shaker

- The more ice that is used the cooler the drink will be but too much ice, especially if crushed, will dilute the drink
- Crushed ice cools a drink more, and more quickly, than cracked ice
- With very few exceptions, always strain cocktails that have been shaken to remove the ice, fragments of fruit flesh or other particles which might mar the appearance of the drink
- Always use clean ice and do not use the same ice for different types of drinks as any liquid adhering to the surface will taint them
- Generally, clear drinks are stirred, while those containing fruit juices, egg white or cream (i.e. ingredients which make a drink cloudy) are shaken (or mixed in a blender)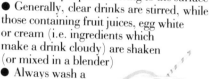
- Always wash a shaker or mixing glass and stirrer between using for different types of drinks
- Keep a container of warm water handy for rinsing spoons etc.
- Serve stars with drinks that contain a lot of ice, or if the rim of the glass has been frosted
- When first making a drink, follow the recipe. However, taste is subjective and if you feel that it contains too much of this or not enough of that for your taste, adjust it to your liking.

Special Preparation of Ice and Sugar

Cracked ice: to prepare cracked ice, put some ice in a strong polythene bag. Bring down sharply on a firm surface, or crack with a heavy implement, such as a wooden rolling pin. Alternatively, use a food processor. Crushed ice can be made in the same way, but broken up more finely. There are also special mechanical ice crushers available.

Powdered sugar: to make powdered sugar, briefly grind granulated sugar in a blender or food processor.

Simple sugar syrup: to make sugar syrup, dissolve powdered sugar in an equal amount of water. This will dissolve more quickly and readily than ordinary sugar in drinks that are not stirred.

Decorations

The look of a drink is very important. With a few, such as Old Fashioned, the decoration is an integral part of the recipe, but in the majority of cases they can be varied according to what is available. However, do try to keep them appropriate to the type and flavour of the drink, for instance, oranges with an orange-flavoured drink. If canned fruits are used, they must be very well drained, otherwise their sweetness will upset the balance of flavours in the drink.

Equipment for Cocktails

The items listed below may not all be absolutely vital, and there is some scope for improvisation, but they will make cocktail-making easier, and probably more successful.

Cocktail shaker: the 'proper' cocktail shakers are usually made of stainless steel, have a strainer and are in two parts.

Screw-top jar: one with a neck wide enough for ice cubes can be used quite successfully in place of a standard cocktail shaker.

Strainer: The traditional ones are made of stainless steel and have a flat, not curved, surface with the holes in, and a springy wire edge.

Measure
Mixing glass
Long-handled spoon for stirring
Teaspoon
Tablespoon
A glass for hot water in which to rinse the spoons

Corkscrew
Bottle opener
Closure for bottle of sparkling wine
Ice bucket or similar insulated container
Tongs for ice
Small, sharp stainless steel knife
Small chopping board
Fruit juice squeezer
Electric blender
Ice crusher
Cocktail sticks
Straws
Beer mats
Tea towel, cloth or paper towels

Stocking the Bar

As with cooking, the quality of the basic ingredients will be reflected in the quality of the product that is made. If the budget is limited, concentrate on quality rather than variety and take advantage of miniatures.

The drinks which will be most useful are:

gin ✓
whisky ✓
vodka ✓
white rum ✓
dark rum ✓
brandy ✓
crème de menthe ✓

curaçao
Cointreau ✓
Grand Marnier ✓
Galliano
Amaretto di Saronno ✓
cherry brandy
dry vermouth ✓

flute

highball

cocktail glass

cocktail glass

old-fashioned

Paris goblet

sweet vermouth
Angostura bitters
soda water
tonic water
lemonade ✓
ginger ale ✓

unsweetened fruit juices—
   especially lime and orange (lime
   is available in bottles, others in
   cartons)
lemons
oranges
cocktail cherries of various colours
olives
sprigs of mint

A greater choice can be offered if the following are also included:

Benedictine
Chartreuse—green and yellow
Tequila
✓ Drambuie
✓ crème de cacao
Irish or Bourbon whiskey

apricot brandy
sparkling wine
orange bitters
egg white
double cream
coconut cream
grenadine

Glasses

The actual authenticity of the style or shape of a glass is really not all that important. What is important is that the glass should be spotlessly clean, free from any detergent or odour—if glasses are stored upside down the air trapped in the bowl will become stale and affect the smell and taste of a drink. If glasses have been stored upside down for any length of time, rinse them before use. When making a drink, choose a glass that will be no more than two-thirds full when both the ice and the drink have been added.

The general types of glasses which will be needed are:

Cocktail glasses—these have a capacity of about 120 ml/4 fl oz, are stemmed and classically 'V'shaped, although available in other shapes.

Old Fashioned—or a tumbler, traditionally with sloping sides, that holds about 175–250 ml/6–8 fl oz.

Highball—tall, straight-sided tumbler holding about 350 ml/12 fl oz.

Champagne flute—that is, a stemmed glass with a tall, slim bowl that curves in slightly at the rim. The old-fashioned saucer-shape allowed the bubbles to disappear and the drink to warm up too quickly.

Standard wine glass

Goblets of varying shapes and sizes

flute

goblet

goblet

tumbler

tulip

liqueur

GIN COCKTAILS

Gin has had a very chequered history. It started life as a medicine, descended to the cheap 'mother's ruin' of the working classes, causing the appearance of the notice 'Drunk for 1d. Dead Drunk for 2d. Clean straw for nothing', before evolving to pride of place amongst the spirits as the foundation of many well-known traditional cocktails and thence on to being a fashionable drink for young executives and the like.

It should be pointed out, however, that the spirit drunk by the poor, wretched masses in the early 1700s was not exactly the same drink that graced the shelves of elegant, fashionable cocktail bars to be consumed by 'dizzy young things'. Over the years, it became drier and greatly improved in quality.

Traditional gin-based cocktails include John Collins (Tom Collins should be made with a particular sweeter type of gin called Old Tom), Bronx, White Lady and, of course, Dry Martini—a combination of gin and a dry vermouth (not necessarily the brand called Martini with which there is no connection, the similarity in name being purely coincidental). The proportions of the two ingredients is the subject of often heated discussions—some advocate that three-quarters gin and one-quarter vermouth should be used, others that the ratio should be seven to one, while others claim that the best Martini is made with no more than one part of dry vermouth to 12 of gin. No-one can be right or wrong as it is purely a matter of taste—the higher the proportion of gin, the drier the drink. The addition of an olive, or lemon peel, either added directly to the drink at the last minute or merely squeezed over the surface, imparts a further subtle flavour. A Sweet Martini cocktail is made not with a high proportion of dry vermouth, but one made with sweet vermouth. Gin and French and Gin and It are made with the same ingredients as Martinis but they are simply poured together over ice; dry vermouth is used for the French version, sweet or red vermouth for the Italian.

By common usage, the name of gin on its own refers to a particular type of gin—London Dry. But other types do exist: Plymouth gin is slightly more aromatic than London Dry while Dutch, Hollands or Geneva is the most highly flavoured. Too dominant for cocktails, it is drunk chilled, neat from small glasses.

Gin Fizz

GIN FIZZ

4 ice cubes, cracked
1 measure gin
2 tablespoons lemon juice
1 teaspoon sugar syrup
½ egg white
1 teaspoon crème de menthe
soda water
To decorate:
sprig of mint
1 slice lemon

Put the ice into a cocktail shaker or screw-top jar and add the gin, lemon juice, sugar syrup, egg white and crème de menthe. Shake to mix. Strain into a tall glass. Top up with soda water and decorate with the mint and lemon.

Serves 1, Preparation time: 4 minutes

GIN SLING

juice of ½ lemon
2 teaspoons powdered sugar
1 measure gin
dash of Angostura bitters
2-3 ice cubes
mineral or soda water

Mix the lemon juice, sugar, gin and bitters together in a tumbler. Add the ice cubes and top up with mineral or soda water.

Serves 1, Preparation time: 3 minutes

HORSE'S NECK

long spiral of lemon peel
3 ice cubes, cracked
1½ measures gin
dry ginger ale

Hang the lemon peel down the side of a tall glass. Add the ice and pour the gin over. Top up with dry ginger ale.

Serves 1, Preparation time: 2 minutes

WHITE HORSES

4 ice cubes, cracked
1 egg white
2 teaspoons sugar syrup
1 measure gin
½ measure lemon juice
½ measure crème de menthe
soda water

mint + lemon

Put the ice cubes into a cocktail shaker and add the egg white, sugar syrup, gin, lemon juice and crème de menthe. Shake very well, then strain into a tall glass. Top up with soda and add a straw.

Serves 1, Preparation time: 4 minutes

Opposite, left to right: Horse's Neck; White Horses

ETON BLAZER

lightly beaten egg white
caster sugar
cracked ice
1 measure gin
1 measure kirsch
¼ measure lemon juice
2 teaspoons sugar syrup
soda water
2 dark cherries, stalks joined, or cocktail cherries, to decorate

Dip the rim of a tumbler in lightly beaten egg white then caster sugar. Add the ice, gin, kirsch, lemon juice and sugar syrup. Stir. Top up with soda water and decorate with the cherries draped over the rim.

Serves 1, Preparation time: 5 minutes

MARTINI

FOR A DRY MARTINI:
cracked ice
1 measure gin
2 measures dry vermouth
To decorate:
strip of lemon peel
1 green olive
FOR A SWEET MARTINI:
few drops of orange bitters (optional)
2 measures gin
1 measure sweet vermouth
1 cocktail cherry, to decorate

DRY MARTINI:
Put some cracked ice in a glass. Pour the gin and vermouth over and stir. Hang the strip of lemon peel over the rim of the glass so that one end is in the cocktail or place it in the glass. Add the olive.

SWEET MARTINI:
Shake a few drops of bitters into a glass and swirl it round to coat the sides. Add the gin and vermouth, and stir to mix. Decorate with the cherry.

Serves 1, Preparation time: 5 minutes

PARADISE

2-3 ice cubes, cracked
1 measure gin
½ measure apricot brandy
½ measure unsweetened orange juice
dash of lemon juice
To decorate:
1 slice orange
1 slice lemon

Place the ice cubes in a cocktail shaker or screw-top jar and add the gin, apricot brandy, orange and lemon juices. Shake to mix and strain into a cocktail glass. Decorate with the fruit slices.

Serves 1, Preparation time: 5 minutes

SINGAPORE SLING

1-2 ice cubes, cracked
1 measure gin
½ measure cherry brandy
¼ measure Cointreau
juice of ½ lemon
soda water
To decorate:
1 slice lemon
cocktail cherries
slices of strawberries, if available
1 slice orange

Put the ice into a tall glass. Add the gin, cherry brandy, Cointreau and lemon juice. Stir and top up with soda water. Decorate with the fruits and drink with straws.
Serves 1, Preparation time: 3 minutes

Left to right: Singapore Sling; Eton Blazer; Paradise

RED KISS

3 ice cubes, cracked
1 measure dry vermouth
½ measure gin
½ measure cherry brandy
To decorate:
1 cocktail cherry
spiral of lemon peel

Put the ice cubes into a mixing glass, add the vermouth, gin and cherry brandy and stir well. Strain into a cocktail glass and decorate with the cherry and lemon peel.

Serves 1, Preparation time: 3 minutes

WOODSTOCK

2-3 ice cubes, crushed
1 measure gin
1 measure dry vermouth
¼ measure Cointreau
1 measure unsweetened orange juice
piece of orange peel
1 slice orange

Put the ice into a cocktail shaker and add the gin, vermouth, Cointreau and orange juice. Shake to mix and strain into a cocktail glass. Squeeze the zest from the orange peel over the surface, and decorate with the slice of orange twisted over the rim of the glass.

Serves 1, Preparation time: 3 minutes

Left to right: Pink Lady; Red Kiss

PINK LADY

beaten egg white
caster sugar
2-3 ice cubes, cracked
½ egg white
1 measure gin
1 teaspoon grenadine
1 teaspoon lemon juice

Dip the rim of a small wine goblet in beaten egg white then caster sugar. Put the ice cubes into a cocktail shaker or screw-top jar and add the remaining ingredients. Shake to mix. Strain into the glass.
Serves 1, Preparation time: 4 minutes

STORMY WEATHER

3 ice cubes, cracked
1½ measures gin
½ measure Mandarine Napoléon liqueur
¼ measure dry vermouth
¼ measure sweet vermouth
twist of lemon peel, to decorate

Put the ice cubes into a cocktail shaker or screw-top jar and add the gin, Mandarine Napoléon and vermouths. Shake to mix and strain into a cocktail glass. Add the twist of lemon to serve.
Serves 1, Preparation time: 3 minutes

Left to right: Woodstock; Stormy Weather

BIJOU

3 ice cubes, cracked
1 measure gin
½ measure green Chartreuse
½ measure sweet vermouth
dash of orange bitters
To decorate:
1 green olive
piece of lemon peel

Put the ice cubes into a mixing glass and add the gin, Chartreuse, vermouth and bitters. Stir well and strain into a cocktail glass. Place the olive on a cocktail stick, add to the cocktail and squeeze the zest from the lemon peel over the surface.
Serves 1, Preparation time: 4 minutes

ORANGE BLOSSOM

1 measure gin
1 measure bianco vermouth
1 measure unsweetened orange juice
1-2 ice cubes
1 slice orange, to decorate

Pour the gin, vermouth and orange juice into a cocktail shaker or screw-top jar and shake to mix. Place the ice cubes in a tall narrow tumbler and strain the cocktail over. Twist the slice of orange and use to decorate the rim of the glass.
Serves 1, Preparation time: 3 minutes

COLLINSON

3 ice cubes, cracked
dash of orange bitters
1 measure gin
½ measure dry vermouth
¼ measure kirsch
piece of lemon peel

To decorate:
cocktail cherries
twist of lemon

Put the ice cubes into a measuring glass, then add the bitters, gin, vermouth and kirsch. Stir well together and strain into a cocktail glass. Squeeze the zest from the lemon peel over the surface, and decorate with the cherries and lemon.
Serves 1, Preparation time: 3 minutes

From the front: Collinson; Bijou; Orange Blossom

MILANO

3 ice cubes, cracked
1 measure gin
1 measure Galliano
1 measure lemon juice
cocktail cherry, to decorate

Put the ice cubes into a cocktail shaker or screw-top jar and add the gin, Galliano and lemon juice. Shake to mix. Strain into a cocktail glass and decorate with the cherry.
Serves 1, Preparation time: 3 minutes

ANGEL'S FACE

3 ice cubes, crushed
¾ measure gin
¾ measure apricot brandy
½ measure Calvados

Put the ice into a cocktail shaker or screw-top jar and add the gin, apricot brandy and Calvados. Shake to mix well and strain into a cocktail glass.
Serves 1, Preparation time: 2 minutes

WHITE LADY

2 measures gin
1 measure Cointreau
1 teaspoon lemon juice
about ½ teaspoon egg white

Place the gin, Cointreau, lemon juice and egg white in a cocktail shaker or screw-topped jar. Shake to mix. Strain into a cocktail glass.
Serves 1, Preparation time: 5 minutes

PINK GIN

1-4 drops Angostura bitters
1 measure gin
iced water

Shake the bitters into a cocktail glass and roll it around until the sides are well coated. Add the gin, then iced water to taste.
Serves 1, Preparation time: 5 minutes

BRONX

cracked ice
1 measure gin
1 measure sweet vermouth
1 measure dry vermouth
2 measures fresh orange juice

Place some cracked ice, the gin, sweet and dry vermouth and orange juice in a cocktail shaker or screw-topped jar. Shake to mix. Pour into a small glass, straining the drink if preferred.
Serves 1, Preparation time: 5 minutes

JOHN COLLINS

1 teaspoon caster sugar
1-2 tablespoons lemon juice
cracked ice
1 measure gin
soda water
1 slice lemon

Put the sugar into a tumbler, add the lemon juice and stir until the sugar has dissolved. Add some cracked ice and stir well. Add the gin and stir lightly. Add soda water to taste, then decorate the rim of the tumbler with the slice of lemon.

Serves 1, Preparation time: 5 minutes

From the front, left to right: Milano; Pink Gin; White Lady; John Collins; Angel's Face

VODKA COCKTAILS

Vodka is an ancient spirit, which is believed to have originated in either Russia or Poland. But it is not the Russian or Polish vodka that has suddenly become popular in the last few years, particularly in the making of cocktails. The traditional vodkas have too pronounced a flavour and, often, too high a strength and price. They are drunk neat, as an aperitif, severely chilled and 'knocked back' all in one go: the smashing of the glass against a wall or fire-place afterwards being purely an optional extra. It is these more highly flavoured vodkas that can accompany caviar, smoked sturgeon and salmon, not the 'modern' ones.

These relatively new, almost flavourless vodkas did not exist until a few decades ago, and may never have reached their present prominence if it had not been for a (happy) coincidence in the late 1940s. That coincidence, so the story goes, took place in a bar in Los Angeles where two men with similar problems—each had a drink he could not sell—sat together bemoaning their fate. Then, eureka, they discovered that by combining the two drinks, vodka and ginger beer, and adding a touch of lime and some ice cubes they had created a drink that was not only pleasant but, given the time and place, had terrific commercial potential. The Screwdriver soon followed and the marketing machinery was set in motion to create an image for, and establish the reputation of, vodka. The rise to fame was not exactly meteoric, but by the 1970s it had become extremely popular, especially among younger people, and it was rivalling gin for pride of place in cocktails.

There are several reasons for vodka's success. Being almost flavourless it blends easily with almost any other cocktail ingredient, although to some people this is considered a draw-back as it gives an undetectable 'kick' and does not add any 'character' to a drink. Also, vodka is low in the constituents which not only cause hang-overs but leave tell-tale signs on the breath. The breathalizer bag is not fooled, though, and will detect vodka just as readily as any other spirit, although Western vodkas are slightly lower in alcohol and therefore slightly more can be consumed before the limit is reached.

White Russian

BULLSHOT

2-3 ice cubes
1 measure vodka
2½ measures canned consommé
dash of Tabasco (optional)
1 teaspoon Worcestershire sauce
1 tablespoon lemon juice

Stir all the ingredients together very well. Strain into a glass.
Serves 1, Preparation time: 3 minutes

WHITE RUSSIAN

5 ice cubes, cracked
1 measure vodka
1 measure Tia Maria
1 measure milk or double cream

Put half the ice cubes into a cocktail shaker or screw-top jar and add the vodka, Tia Maria and milk. Shake to mix. Put the remaining ice cubes into a tall narrow glass and strain over the cocktail. Drink with a straw.
Serves 1, Preparation time: 3 minutes

NORMAN CONQUEROR

4 ice cubes, cracked
1 measure vodka
½ measure Calvados
½ measure unsweetened apple juice
dash of Angostura bitters
To decorate:
1 slice orange
1 slice lemon
sprig of mint

Put half the ice cubes into a cocktail shaker or screw-top jar and add the vodka, Calvados, apple juice and bitters. Shake to mix. Put the remaining ice into a tall glass and strain in the cocktail. Decorate with the slices of orange and lemon and the sprig of mint.
Serves 1, Preparation time: 3 minutes

ORANGE MIST

4 ice cubes, cracked
¾ measure vodka
1 measure Irish Mist
2 measures unsweetened orange juice
soda water
1 slice orange, to decorate

Put half the ice cubes into a cocktail shaker or screw-top jar and add the vodka, Irish Mist and orange juice. Shake to mix. Put the remaining ice into a tumbler and pour over the cocktail. Add a splash of soda and decorate the glass with the orange.
Serves 1, Preparation time: 3 minutes
Opposite, left to right: Norman Conqueror; Orange Mist

PERFECT LOVE

3 ice cubes, cracked
1 measure vodka
½ measure Parfait Amour
¼ measure maraschino
twist of lemon peel, to decorate

Put the ice cubes into a small glass and add the remaining ingredients. Stir well, add the twist of lemon peel and drink with a short straw.

Serves 1, Preparation time: 3 minutes

HARVEY WALLBANGER

cracked ice
2 measures fresh orange juice
1 measure vodka
2 teaspoons Galliano

To decorate:
slice of cucumber
twist of orange peel
1 slice pineapple
cocktail cherry

Place some cracked ice in a tumbler. Pour on the fresh orange juice and vodka. Pour on the Galliano and stir well. Decorate with the cucumber, orange peel, pineapple and cocktail cherry, on a cocktail stick.

Serves 1, Preparation time: 5 minutes

LE MANS

2-3 ice cubes, cracked
1 measure Cointreau
½ measure vodka
soda water
1 slice lemon

Put the ice into a tall glass. Add the Cointreau and vodka, stir and top up with soda. Float the slice of lemon on top.
Serves 1, Preparation time: 2 minutes

BEHIND THE WALL

2-3 ice cubes, crushed
1 measure vodka
⅔ measure Mandarine Napoléon liqueur
⅔ measure Galliano
1 measure unsweetened orange juice
ginger ale
1 slice orange, to decorate

Put the ice into a cocktail shaker or screw-top jar and add the vodka, Mandarine Napoléon, Galliano and orange juice. Shake to mix. Strain into a tall glass and top up with ginger ale. Decorate with the orange slice and drink with a straw.
Serves 1, Preparation time: 3 minutes

Left to right: Le Mans; Harvey Wallbanger; Perfect Love; Behind the wall

BLACK RUSSIAN

cracked ice
2 measures vodka
1 measure Kahlúa coffee liqueur

Put some cracked ice in a glass. Add the vodka and Kahlúa and stir.
Serves 1, Preparation time: 5 minutes

SCREWDRIVER

2-3 ice cubes
1 measure vodka
juice of 1 orange

*Put the ice cubes into a tumbler. Add the vodka and orange juice,
and stir lightly.*
Serves 1, Preparation time: 5 minutes

HAIR RAISER

1-2 ice cubes, cracked
1 measure vodka
1 measure sweet vermouth
1 measure tonic water
twists of lemon and lime, to decorate

*Put the ice cubes into a tall narrow tumbler and pour the vodka,
vermouth and tonic over. Stir lightly, serve with a stirrer and
decorate with the lemon and lime.*
Serves 1, Preparation time: 2 minutes

RUSSIAN SECRET

4 ice cubes, cracked
½ measure vodka
½ measure Benedictine
2 measures unsweetened grapefruit juice

*Put half the ice cubes into a cocktail shaker or screw-top jar and
add the vodka, Benedictine and grapefruit juice. Shake to mix. Put
the remaining ice into a glass and strain over the cocktail.*
Serves 1, Preparation time: 2 minutes

MOSCOW MULE

2-3 ice cubes
juice of ½ lime or lemon
twist of lime or lemon peel
1½ measures vodka
ginger beer, to taste
strip of lime or lemon peel, to decorate

*Put the ice cubes in a tall glass. add the juice and peel and stir in
the vodka. Top up with ginger beer to taste and decorate with
slices of lime or lemon.*
Serves 1, Preparation time: 5 minutes
Left to right: Hair Raiser; Moscow Mule; Russian Secret; Black Russian

WHISKY COCKTAILS

Whisky can be made in any part of the world where there is access to grain and a suitable water supply. It is often claimed that the water is the most crucial factor in determining the character, and quality, of a whisky. About 98 per cent of the whisky sold in this country is blended Scotch whisky; this combines the lightness of whisky distilled from a blend of grains with the more positive character of malt whisky. Each brand will be blended to a specific formula that the company feels will do well commercially, while at the same time create a certain image. Some may contain as many as 50 different whiskies and the more expensive, which usually have a more distinct, although not fiery flavour, include a higher proportion of the malt whiskies.

Scotland, though, was not the home of whisky. Ireland is generally accepted as being its birthplace—about 800 years ago. Irish whiskey, spelt with an 'e', is made from a different blend of grains from Scotch—it usually contains barley, malted barley, rye, wheat and sometimes even oats—which contribute towards its distinctive aroma and more mellow flavour. Bourbon whiskey is just one of the 30 or so American whiskies. The grain from which it is made must contain at least 51 per cent corn (maize) which, together with the use of charred white oak casks, gives it its characteristic flavour. Rye whiskey contains at least 51 per cent rye.

Of the spirits, whisky is the least frequently used in cocktails, and those in which it is used are usually of the more straightforward kind—with ginger ale, lemon, lemonade or perhaps just one liqueur. Whisky lovers who throw up their hands in horror at even the inclusion of water, claim that to add anything more flavoursome is tantamount to sacrilege. But the whisky of connoiseurs is malt, particularly single (i.e. unblended) malt, and certainly this is not the whisky to use in cocktails. Also, most of the traditional whisk(e)y-based cocktails emanate from America, so Bourbon or rye would be used. Possibly the most well-known exception is Bonnie Prince Charlie which, unsurprisingly, is Scotch whisky combined with Drambuie, the whisky-based liqueur. The recipe for this drink was given by Bonnie Prince Charlie to his companion, Captain Mackinnon, after his defeat at Culloden in 1746. That is, if legend is to be believed!

Whisky Mac

WHISKY MAC

2-3 ice cubes
1 measure Scotch whisky
1 measure ginger wine

Place the ice cubes in a tumbler. Add the whisky and ginger wine.
Serves 1, Preparation time: 3 minutes

RITZ OLD-FASHIONED

lightly beaten egg white
caster sugar
3 ice cubes, crushed
1½ measures Bourbon whiskey
½ measure Grand Marnier
dash of lemon juice
dash of Angostura bitters
To decorate:
1 slice orange or lemon
1 cocktail cherry

Dip the rim of an Old-Fashioned glass in the beaten egg white then caster sugar. Put the ice into a cocktail shaker or screw-top jar and add the Bourbon, Grand Marnier, lemon juice and bitters. Shake together, then strain into the glass. Decorate with the orange or lemon and the cherry.
Serves 1, Preparation time: 5 minutes

CLUB

3 ice cubes, cracked
2 dashes Angostura bitters
1 measure Scotch whisky
dash of grenadine
To decorate:
twist of lemon peel
1 cocktail cherry

Put the ice into a mixing glass. Add the bitters then the whisky and grenadine. Stir well. Strain into a cocktail glass and decorate.
Serves 1, Preparation time: 3 minutes

CAPRICORN

4 ice cubes, cracked
1 measure Bourbon whiskey
½ measure apricot brandy
½ measure lemon juice
2 measures unsweetened orange juice
1 slice orange, to decorate

Put half the ice cubes into a cocktail shaker or screw-top jar and add the whiskey, apricot brandy, lemon and orange juices. Shake to mix. Put the remaining ice cubes into an Old-Fashioned glass and strain on the cocktail. Decorate with the slice of orange.
Serves 1, Preparation time: 3 minutes
Left to right: Capricorn; Club; Ritz Old-Fashioned

GODFATHER

2 ice cubes
1 measure Scotch whisky
1 measure Amaretto di Saronno

Put the ice into a small tumbler, pour over the whisky and Amaretto and stir.
Serves 1, Preparation time: 2 minutes

ROYAL SCOT

3 ice cubes, cracked
1 measure Scotch whisky
½ measure Drambuie
½ measure green Chartreuse
1 cocktail cherry, to decorate

Put the ice cubes into a cocktail shaker or screw-top jar and add the whisky, Drambuie and Chartreuse. Shake to mix. Strain into a cocktail glass. Spear the cherry with a cocktail stick and add to the drink.
Serves 1, Preparation time: 3 minutes

Left to right: Godfather; Rob Roy

ROB ROY

1 ice cube, cracked
1 measure Scotch whisky
½ measure dry vermouth
dash of Angostura bitters
twist of lemon peel, to decorate

Mix the ice cube, whisky, vermouth and bitters together. Strain into
a cocktail glass and decorate the rim with the lemon peel.
Serves 1, Preparation time: 3 minutes

SUPERMAC

2 ice cubes, cracked
1 measure Scotch whisky
½ measure ginger wine
½ measure lemon juice
dash of maraschino

Put the ice cubes into a cocktail shaker or screw-top jar and add the
remaining ingredients. Shake to mix. Strain into a cocktail glass.
Serves 1, Preparation time: 2 minutes

Left to right: Royal Scot; Supermac

WHISKY DAISY

3 ice cubes, crushed
1 egg white
½ measure lemon juice
1 measure Scotch whisky
1 teaspoon Pernod
2 dashes grenadine
soda water
1 slice lemon, to decorate

Put the ice into a cocktail shaker or screw-top jar and add the egg white, lemon juice, whisky, Pernod and grenadine. Shake to mix. Strain into an Old-Fashioned glass, top up with soda water and add the slice of lemon.

Serves 1, Preparation time: 3 minutes

OLD-FASHIONED

1 sugar lump
1-2 drops Angostura bitters
1-2 ice cubes
1 measure whisky

Put the sugar into a tumbler, shake in the bitters and stir until the sugar has dissolved. Add the ice cubes and stir. Add the whisky.

Serves 1, Preparation time: 5 minutes

NEW YORKER

2-3 ice cubes, cracked
1 measure Scotch whisky
1 teaspoon unsweetened lime juice
1 teaspoon powdered sugar
piece of lemon peel

Put the ice cubes in a cocktail shaker or screw-top jar and add the whisky, lime juice and sugar. Shake to mix. Strain into a cocktail glass. Squeeze the zest from the lemon peel over the surface.

Serves 1, Preparation time: 3 minutes

MANHATTAN

cracked ice
2 measures rye whiskey
1 measure sweet vermouth
dash of Angostura bitters

To decorate:
1 cocktail cherry
strip of lemon peel

Put some cracked ice into a glass. Mix together the whiskey, vermouth and bitters, then pour over the ice. Stir once. Add the cherry and lemon peel on a cocktail stick, to decorate.

Serves 1, Preparation time: 5 minutes

Left to right: New Yorker; Manhattan; Old-Fashioned

MINT JULEP

3 sprigs mint
½ teaspoon caster sugar
1 tablespoon soda water
2-3 ice cubes, crushed
1 measure Bourbon whiskey
sprig of mint, to decorate

Crush the mint with the sugar in a tumbler and rub it around the sides of the glass. Discard the mint. Dissolve the sugar in the soda water, add the ice and pour over the Bourbon. Do not stir. Decorate with the sprig of mint.
Serves 1, Preparation time: 3 minutes

WHISKY SOUR

2-3 teaspoons lemon juice
1 teaspoon caster sugar
cracked ice
1 measure whisky

In a whisky tumbler stir together the lemon juice and caster sugar, until the sugar has dissolved. Add some cracked ice and stir to coat with the liquid. Add the whisky and stir lightly.
Serves 1, Preparation time: 5 minutes

Left to right: Mint Julep; Whisky Sour

RUSTY NAIL

2-3 ice cubes
1 measure Scotch whisky
½ measure Drambuie
twist of lemon peel, to decorate

Put the ice into a small tumbler and pour over the whisky. Pour the Drambuie over the back of a teaspoon on top of the whisky. Decorate the rim of the glass with a twist of lemon peel.
Serves 1, Preparation time: 3 minutes

BRAINSTORM

3 ice cubes
1 measure Irish whiskey
¼ measure dry vermouth
¼ measure Benedictine
1 olive, to decorate

Put the ice into an Old-Fashioned glass and pour over the whiskey, vermouth and Benedictine. Stir and decorate with the olive.
Serves 1, Preparation time: 2 minutes

Left to right: Rusty Nail; Brainstorm

RUM COCKTAILS

Rum has a strange mixture of associations—from smugglers risking ship-wreck off the Cornish coast and capture by the merciless militia men, or free tipple that kept the British Navy happy, to wealthy planters relaxing on sunny verandas leisurely sipping long fruit-bedecked concoctions.

Rum is distilled from sugar cane and is made wherever this crop is grown, although the West Indies and mainlands around the Caribbean have the vast majority of commercial production.

Originally, there were great differences in the flavours and colours of rums made in different areas. For example, a rum from Jamaica, as distributed by the British Navy, would be dark golden with a pungent flavour, while one from Barbados or Trinidad would be light and dry. The Demerara or Guyana rums were the darkest and heaviest but with less pungency than a Jamaican, and from Cuba came light, or as they are more popularly and accurately known, white rums.

Nowadays, although it is still possible to buy rums that are made by the old, traditional methods and therefore exhibit the regional characteristics, the majority which line the supermarket and off-licence shelves will be mass-produced and more consistent in flavour and colour. The type of rum which has really become popular in recent years is white rum—lighter in style it found favour amongst younger drinkers often as a result of a Continental holiday and the sampling of Daiquiris, Pina Coladas and Cubre Libres. Also, with their lighter flavour white rums blend easily with many other different flavours. The darker styles seem to have a particular affinity for fruit juices, especially lime, and seem to conjure up connotations of Caribbean life. It is also a particularly warming spirit and is frequently used in hot punches or drinks.

Planter's Cocktail

PLANTER'S COCKTAIL

3 ice cubes, cracked
1 measure dark rum
½ measure unsweetened orange juice
½ measure lemon juice
2 dashes Angostura bitters
1 teaspoon powdered sugar

To decorate:
pineapple cubes
slices of banana
twist of orange

Put the ice cubes into a cocktail shaker or screw-top jar and add the rum, orange juice, lemon juice, bitters and sugar. Shake to mix. Strain into a large cocktail glass. Decorate with the pineapple, banana and orange twist.

Serves 1, Preparation time: 4 minutes

ZOMBIE

3 ice cubes, cracked
1 measure dark rum
1 measure white rum
½ measure apricot brandy
2 measures unsweetened pineapple juice
1 tablespoon unsweetened lime juice
2 teaspoons powdered sugar

To decorate:
sprig of mint
cocktail cherries
pineapple cubes
powdered sugar

Place a tall glass in the freezer so the outside becomes frosted. Put the ice into a cocktail shaker or screw-top jar. Add the rums, apricot brandy, fruit juices and sugar. Shake to mix. Pour into the glass without straining. Put the mint, cherries and pineapple on to a cocktail stick and place across the top of the glass. Sprinkle the powdered sugar over the drink and drink with a straw.

Serves 1, Preparation time: 5 minutes

CUBRE LIBRE

2-3 ice cubes
1½ measures dark rum
juice of ½ lime (or 1 tablespoon unsweetened lime juice)
Coca-cola
slice of lime, to decorate

Place the ice cubes in a tall tumbler and pour over the rum and lime juice. Stir to mix. Top up with Coca-cola, twist the slice of lime to decorate and drink with a straw.

Serves 1, Preparation time: 3 minutes

Left to right: Cubre Libre; Waterloo; Zombie

WATERLOO

lightly beaten egg white
caster sugar
5 ice cubes, cracked
¾ measure white rum
¾ measure Mandarine Napoléon liqueur
1½ measures unsweetened orange juice
soda water
orange peel, to decorate

Dip the rim of a goblet in the beaten egg white, then caster sugar.
Put half the ice cubes into a cocktail shaker or screw-top jar and
add the rum, Mandarine Napoléon and orange juice. Shake to mix.
Put the remaining ice cubes into the goblet and strain over the
cocktail. Top up with soda, decorate with the orange peel and drink
with a straw.

Serves 1, Preparation time: 4 minutes

COCO LOCO

¾ measure white rum
¾ measure Tequila
½ measure vodka
1 measure coconut cream
1 tablespoon lemon juice
3 ice cubes, cracked
To decorate:
twist of lemon
cocktail cherries

Pour the rum, Tequila, vodka, coconut cream and lemon juice into a blender. Mix for 15 seconds. Put the ice cubes into a large goblet and pour over the drink. Decorate with the lemon and cherries and drink with a straw.
Serves 1, Preparation time: 3 minutes

EL DORADO

strip of orange peel
desiccated coconut
3 ice cubes, cracked
1 measure white rum
1 measure advocaat
1 measure crème de cacao
1 teaspoon grated coconut or ½ teaspoon desiccated coconut
To decorate:
1 slice orange
cocktail cherries

Wipe around the rim of a large cocktail glass with the orange peel, then dip it in desiccated coconut. Put the ice into a cocktail shaker or screw-top jar and add the rum, advocaat, crème de cacao and grated or desiccated coconut. Shake to mix. Strain into the glass, then decorate with orange and cherries, and drink with a straw.
Serves 1, Preparation time: 5 minutes

MAI TAI

lightly beaten egg white
caster sugar
1 measure white rum
½ measure unsweetened orange juice
½ measure unsweetened lime juice
3 ice cubes, crushed
To decorate:
cocktail cherries
pineapple cubes
orange slices

Dip the rim of a stemmed glass in the beaten egg white, then the caster sugar. Put the rum, orange juice and lime juice into a cocktail shaker or screw-top jar. Shake to mix. Put the ice into the glass and pour over the cocktail. Decorate with the cherries, pineapple and orange slices and drink with a short straw.
Serves 1, Preparation time: 5 minutes

From top to bottom: El Dorado; Coco Loco; Mai Tai

DAIQUIRI

3 ice cubes, cracked
1 measure lime cordial or juice
3 measures white rum

Put the cracked ice into a glass, pour over the lime cordial or juice then the rum and stir lightly.
Serves 1, Preparation time: 3 minutes

BANANA DAIQUIRI

3 ice cubes, cracked
1 measure white rum
1 measure dark rum
2 measures orange juice
½ measure banana liqueur
½ small banana
1 measure single cream (optional)
To decorate:
2 cocktail cherries
1 slice pineapple

Put the cracked ice in a tall goblet. Put the rums, orange juice, liqueur, banana and cream, if using, into a blender and blend for 30 seconds. Pour into the glass and decorate with the fruit.
Serves 1, Preparation time: 5 minutes

EDGEMOOR

3 ice cubes, cracked
1 measure dark rum
1 measure white rum
1 measure Irish Mist
3 measures fresh pineapple juice
1 teaspoon lime cordial
soda water
twisted strip of orange or lemon peel, to decorate

Put the cracked ice into a cocktail shaker or screw-top jar with the rums, Irish Mist, pineapple juice and lime cordial. Shake to mix. Strain into a tall glass, top up with soda water and decorate.
Serves 1, Preparation time: 5 minutes

FLORIDA SKIES

cracked ice
1 measure white rum
¼ measure lime juice
½ measure pineapple juice
soda water
1 slice lime or cucumber, to decorate

Put some cracked ice in a tall glass. Put the rum, lime and pineapple juices in a cocktail shaker or screw-topped jar. Shake lightly. Strain into the glass and top up with soda water. Decorate with the lime or cucumber slice on a stick parasol.
Serves 1, Preparation time: 3 minutes
Left to right: Edgemoor;·Banana Daiquiri; Florida Skies

TEMPO

3 ice cubes, cracked
1 measure white rum
1 measure unsweetened lime juice
½ measure crème de cacao
dash of Angostura bitters
lemonade
1 slice lime, to decorate

Put the ice cubes into a tall glass and add the rum, lime juice, crème de cacao and bitters. Stir, then top up with lemonade. Decorate with the lime slice.

Serves 1, Preparation time: 2 minutes

SERENADE

6 ice cubes, crushed
1 measure white rum
½ measure Amaretto di Saronno
½ measure coconut cream
2 measures unsweetened pineapple juice
pineapple slices, to decorate

Put half the ice into a blender and add the rum, Amaretto, coconut cream and pineapple juice and blend for 20 seconds. Put the remaining ice into a tall glass and pour over the cocktail. Serve decorated with the pineapple and drink with a long straw.

Serves 1, Preparation time: 23 seconds

PINA COLADA

cracked ice
1 measure white rum
2 measures cream of coconut milk
2 measures fresh pineapple juice
To decorate:
1 cocktail cherry
slice of orange or canned or fresh pineapple

Place some cracked ice, the rum, coconut milk and pineapple juice in a cocktail shaker or screw-topped jar. Shake lightly to mix. Strain into a large glass and decorate with the fruit.

Serves 1, Preparation time: 5 minutes

SUMMERTIME

3 ice cubes, cracked
1½ measures Orange Nassau liqueur
½ measure dark rum
2 teaspoons lemon juice
twist of lemon, to decorate

Put the ice cubes into a cocktail shaker or screw-top jar and add the Orange Nassau, rum and lemon juice. Shake to mix. Strain into a cocktail glass and decorate with the twist of lemon.

Serves 1, Preparation time: 3 minutes

Left to right: Serenade; Summertime; Tempo

ROSALIE

2-3 ice cubes
1 measure white rum
½ measure dry vermouth
¼ measure apricot brandy
dash of unsweetened lime juice

Put the ice into a cocktail shaker or screw-top jar. Add the remaining ingredients. Shake to mix. Strain into a cocktail glass.

Serves 1, Preparation time: 3 minutes

JOLLY ROGER

5 ice cubes, cracked
1 measure dark rum
1 measure Galliano
½ measure apricot brandy
3 measures unsweetened orange juice
To decorate:
1 piece apricot
1 slice orange
1 slice lemon

Put half the ice cubes into a cocktail shaker or screw-top jar. Add the rum, Galliano, apricot brandy and orange juice. Shake to mix. Put the remaining ice into a tall glass and strain over the cocktail. Decorate with the apricot, orange and lemon slices.

Serves 1, Preparation time: 5 minutes

Left to right: Jolly Roger; Rosalie

PINK TREASURE

2 ice cubes, cracked
1 measure white rum
1 measure cherry brandy
bitter lemon or soda water (optional)
twist of lemon, to decorate

Put the ice cubes, rum and brandy into a small glass. Add a splash of bitter lemon or soda water. Decorate with the twist of lemon.
Serves 1, Preparation time: 2 minutes

BOMBAY SMASH

5 ice cubes, crushed
1 measure dark rum
1 measure Malibu
3 measures unsweetened pineapple juice
2 teaspoons lemon juice
¼ measure Triple Sec
pineapple cubes
1 slice lemon

Put half the ice into a cocktail shaker or screw-top jar. Add the rum, Malibu, pineapple juice, lemon juice and Triple Sec. Shake to mix. Put the remaining ice into a tall glass and strain over the cocktail. Decorate with the pineapple cubes and lemon and drink with a straw.
Serves 1, Preparation time: 4 minutes

Left to right: Pink Treasure; Bombay Smash

BRANDY COCKTAILS

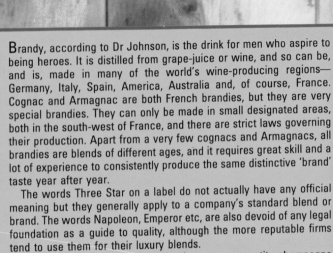

Brandy, according to Dr Johnson, is the drink for men who aspire to being heroes. It is distilled from grape-juice or wine, and so can be, and is, made in many of the world's wine-producing regions—Germany, Italy, Spain, America, Australia and, of course, France. Cognac and Armagnac are both French brandies, but they are very special brandies. They can only be made in small designated areas, both in the south-west of France, and there are strict laws governing their production. Apart from a very few cognacs and Armagnacs, all brandies are blends of different ages, and it requires great skill and a lot of experience to consistently produce the same distinctive 'brand' taste year after year.

The words Three Star on a label do not actually have any official meaning but they generally apply to a company's standard blend or brand. The words Napoleon, Emperor etc, are also devoid of any legal foundation as a guide to quality, although the more reputable firms tend to use them for their luxury blends.

If either fine champagne, grande champagne or petite champagne appears on the label it does not denote any connection with the sparkling white wine of the same name. It indicates that the product within the bottle has been made from grapes grown in the very best areas of cognac. A fine champagne cognac is, therefore, one of the very best. When making cocktails it is not worth using a fine champagne cognac or other luxury blend, but it is certainly worth buying a reasonable Three Star, or equivalent, cognac. Cheap brandies invariably taste cheap and will transfer their cheapness to any drink made with them.

Creole Punch

BETWEEN THE SHEETS

2-3 ice cubes, cracked
½ measure brandy
½ measure white rum
½ measure Cointreau
1 tablespoon unsweetened orange juice

Put the ice into a cocktail shaker or screw-top jar. Add the remaining ingredients and shake to mix. Strain into a cocktail glass.

Serves 1, Preparation time: 3 minutes

ALEXANDER

2-3 ice cubes, cracked
1 measure brandy
1 measure crème de cacao (e.g. Tia Maria)
1 measure cream

Put the ice into a cocktail shaker or screw-top jar and add the brandy, crème de cacao and cream. Shake well to mix thoroughly and strain into a cocktail glass.

Serves 1, Preparation time: 3 minutes

CREOLE PUNCH

5 ice cubes, crushed
1½ measures port
½ measure brandy
2 teaspoons lemon juice
lemonade

To decorate:
1 slice orange
1 slice lemon
pineapple chunks
cocktail cherries

Put half the ice into a cocktail shaker or screw-top jar and add the port, brandy and lemon juice. Shake to mix. Put the remaining ice into a goblet, pour the cocktail over and top up with lemonade. Decorate with the fruit.

Serves 1, Preparation time: 5 minutes

BRANDY DAISY

2-3 ice cubes, cracked
1 measure brandy
¼ measure lemon juice
2 teaspoons grenadine
soda water (optional)
cocktail cherries, to decorate

Put the ice cubes into a cocktail shaker or screw-top jar and add the brandy, lemon juice and grenadine. Shake to mix and strain into a glass. Top up with soda water if liked. Decorate with the cherries.

Serves 1, Preparation time: 4 minutes

BRANDY FIX

1 teaspoon powdered sugar
1 teaspoon water
1 measure brandy
½ measure cherry brandy
juice of ½ lemon
crushed ice
1 slice lemon, to decorate

Dissolve the sugar in the water in a small tumbler then add the brandy, cherry brandy and lemon juice. Stir to mix. Fill the glass with crushed ice, float the lemon slice on top and drink with a straw.

Serves 1, Preparation time: 3 minutes

Left to right: Brandy Fix; Between the Sheets; Alexander; Brandy Daisy

BRANDY SMASH

4 sprigs mint
1 teaspoon powdered sugar
2 ice cubes, cracked
1 measure brandy
soda water

Crush the mint and sugar together in an Old-Fashioned glass, and rub the mix around the sides of the glass. Discard the mint. Add the ice cubes and brandy then a splash of soda water.
Serves 1, Preparation time: 4 minutes

LEO

2-3 ice cubes, crushed
1 measure brandy
1½ measures unsweetened orange juice
½ measure Amaretto di Saronno
soda water
1 teaspoon Campari

Put the ice cubes into a cocktail shaker. Add the brandy, orange juice and Amaretto. Shake. Strain into a tall glass and add soda water and Campari.
Serves 1, Preparation time: 4 minutes

Left to right: Leo; Brandy Smash

BACCHUS

4 ice cubes, cracked
2 measures brandy
1 measure apricot brandy
1 measure unsweetened lime juice
spiral of lime peel, to decorate

Put half the ice cubes into a cocktail shaker or screw-top jar and add the brandy, apricot brandy and lime juice. Shake to mix. Put the remaining ice into a small goblet and pour over the cocktail. Decorate with the lime peel.

Serves 1, Preparation time: 4 minutes

HONEYMOON

2-3 ice cubes, cracked
1 measure Calvados
½ measure Benedictine
2 teaspoons unsweetened orange juice
1 teaspoon Cointreau

Put the ice cubes into a cocktail shaker or screw-top jar and add the Calvados, Benedictine and orange juice. Shake to mix. Strain into a cocktail glass. Pour the Cointreau on to the surface but do not stir.

Serves 1, Preparation time: 4 minutes

Left to right: Bacchus; Honeymoon

SIDECAR

2-3 ice cubes
1 measure brandy
½ measure Cointreau
½ measure lemon juice
twist of lemon peel, to decorate

Crack the ice cubes and put into a cocktail shaker or screw-topped jar. Add the brandy, Cointreau and lemon juice and shake lightly to mix. Strain into a cocktail glass and decorate with lemon peel.
Serves 1, Preparation time: 5 minutes

FRENCHMAN

2-3 ice cubes, cracked
1 measure brandy
½ measure green Chartreuse
juice of 1 small lemon

Put the ice cubes into a cocktail shaker or screw-top jar and add the brandy, Chartreuse and lemon juice. Shake to mix and pour into a cocktail glass.
Serves 1, Preparation time: 3 minutes

Left to right: Sidecar; Frenchman

KLONDIKE

2 ice cubes, cracked
1 measure Calvados
¾ measure dry vermouth
2 dashes Angostura bitters

Put the ice cubes into a cocktail shaker or screw-top jar and add the Calvados, vermouth and bitters. Shake. Strain into a cocktail glass.
Serves 1, Preparation time: 3 minutes

SUNDOWNER

2-3 ice cubes, cracked
1 measure brandy
1 teaspoon lemon juice
1 teaspoon unsweetened orange juice
½ measure Van der Hum liqueur
twist of orange peel, to decorate

Place the ice in a cocktail shaker or screw-top jar. Add the brandy, lemon juice, orange juice and liqueur and shake to mix. Strain into a cocktail glass and decorate with orange peel.
Serves 1, Preparation time: 5 minutes

Left to right: Klondike; Sundowner

ROYAL WEDDING

2-3 ice cubes, cracked
1 measure brandy
½ measure peach brandy
½ measure kirsch
2 measures unsweetened orange juice
soda water
To decorate:
peach slices
orange slices
cocktail cherries

Put the ice cubes into a cocktail shaker or screw-top jar. Add the brandy, peach brandy, kirsch and orange juice and shake to mix. Pour into a tall glass and top up with soda water. Decorate with the peach slices, orange slices and cherries.
Serves 1, Preparation time: 5 minutes

SCORPION

5 ice cubes, crushed
1 measure brandy
½ measure white rum
½ measure dark rum
2 measures unsweetened orange juice
2 teaspoons Amaretto di Saronno
2-3 dashes Angostura bitters
To decorate:
1 slice orange
1 slice lemon

Put half the ice into a cocktail shaker or screw-top jar and add the brandy, rums, orange juice, Amaretto and bitters. Shake to mix. Put the remaining ice into a goblet and strain over the cocktail. Decorate with the orange and lemon slices and drink with a straw.
Serves 1, Preparation time: 4 minutes

HARVARD COOLER

3 ice cubes, crushed
1 measure Calvados
1 measure unsweetened orange juice
1 teaspoon powdered sugar
ginger ale
To decorate:
spiral of lemon peel
1 slice orange
3 pieces preserved ginger

Put the ice cubes into a cocktail shaker or screw-top jar and add the Calvados, orange juice and sugar. Shake to mix. Strain into a tall glass. Top up with ginger ale. Drape the lemon peel over the rim of the glass. Twist the slice of orange and arrange it on a cocktail stick with the ginger.
Serves 1, Preparation time: 3 minutes

Left to right: Royal Wedding; Harvard Cooler; Scorpion

Although spirits form the basis of the majority of cocktails, there are some which are 'spiritless' but which, nonetheless, are alcoholic.

Vermouth in all its styles—sweet, dry, rosso and bianco—and other aperitifs such as Campari, St Raphael, Punt e Mes, Dubonnet, Amer Picon, Pernod and sherries, port and Madeira all play their part in the creation of cocktails. But it is liqueurs which are indispensible to any cocktail collection, as well as cold cups and punches. Liqueurs are distillations or infusions of herbs, fruits or spices in alcohol. On their own, they are traditionally drunk after a meal, particularly dinner, theoretically by the ladies (the gentlemen partaking of the port and cognac) and it is probably in cocktails and long drinks, to which they add flavour, depth, character and usually sweetness, that they are now far more widely consumed.

There are hundreds of liqueurs, with some falling into generic groups, such as cherry brandies, while others are known by particular brand names, such as Chartreuse, Benedictine or Southern Comfort. Many are centuries old and there are quite a number which have monastic connections, but in recent years there have been quite a few new liqueurs. These have often been created with commerce in mind and once one of a type has been launched, others follow. Probably the most notable of these have been the cream-based products which did not really exist before 1975, and now there are many, with still more appearing all the time. The cream is usually blended with Scotch or Irish whisk(e)y or brandy and may contain other flavourings such as coffee or chocolate.

Some liqueurs are almost universally well known, appearing wherever liqueurs are served. Drambuie is one such liqueur, but there are others which, although they have been in existence for quite a while have remained in comparative obscurity, only recently coming to popular attention with the increasing interest in cocktails. For example, Galliano, the bright yellow-green liqueur with a flavour redolent of herbs and liquorice, has been available since the late 1800s but it was not until it received a lot of publicity as a cocktail ingredient that it was widely known outside its native Italy. Tequila is another ingredient that was little known, outside its home in Mexico except by its reputation for being made from the juice of the cactus plant. Then came the cocktails, first the Margarita, then Tequila Sunrise and now many, many more.

Barbera

BROOKLYN BOMBER

5 ice cubes, cracked
½ measure Tequila
½ measure Triple Sec
½ measure cherry brandy
½ measure Galliano
1 measure lemon juice
To decorate:
1 slice orange
1 cocktail cherry

Put half the ice cubes into a cocktail shaker or screw-top jar and add the Tequila, Triple Sec, cherry brandy, Galliano and lemon juice. Shake to mix. Put the remaining ice into a tall glass and pour over the drink. Decorate with the orange and cherry and drink with a straw.

Serves 1, Preparation time: 3 minutes

MARGARITA

a little lemon juice
finely ground sea salt
1½ measures Tequila
1 measure Triple Sec
1-2 tablespoons lemon or lime juice
cracked ice

Dip the rim of a chilled glass in lemon juice, then in the salt. Place the Tequila, Triple Sec, lemon or lime juice and cracked ice in a cocktail shaker or screw-topped jar. Shake well to mix. Pour into the glass.

Serves 1, Preparation time: 5 minutes

BARBERA

5 ice cubes, cracked
1 measure Bourbon
¾ measure Drambuie
¼ measure Amaretto di Saronno
2 dashes orange bitters
twist of lemon peel
1 slice orange, to decorate

Put half the ice cubes into a mixing glass and add the Bourbon, Drambuie, Amaretto and bitters. Stir to mix. Put the remaining ice cubes into a tumbler and strain over the cocktail. Squeeze the zest from the lemon peel over the surface and decorate with the orange.

Serves 1, Preparation time: 3 minutes

GRASSHOPPER

1 measure crème de cacao
1 measure crème de menthe

Pour the crème de cacao into a small glass. Pour the crème de menthe gently over the back of a teaspoon so that it floats on the surface. Drink with a short straw.

Serves 1, Preparation time: 3 minutes

AMERICANO

cracked ice
1 measure Campari
2 measures sweet vermouth
soda water
twist of lemon peel, to decorate

Put some cracked ice into a tumbler, pour the Campari and vermouth over. Stir to mix. Top up with soda water to taste. Decorate with the lemon peel.

Serves 1, Preparation time: 5 minutes

Grasshopper; Brooklyn Bomber; Margarita

TEQUILA SUNRISE

5-6 ice cubes
1 measure Tequila
2½ measures unsweetened orange juice
2 teaspoons grenadine

Crack half the ice and put in a cocktail shaker or screw-top jar. Add the Tequila and orange juice and shake to mix. Put the remaining ice into a narrow tumbler and strain the Tequila over. Slowly pour in the grenadine and allow to settle. Just before serving, stir once.
Serves 1, Preparation time: 5 minutes

SICILIAN KISS

5 ice cubes, cracked
1 measure Southern Comfort
1 measure Amaretto di Saronno

Put half the ice cubes into a cocktail shaker or screw-top jar and add the Southern Comfort and Amaretto. Shake to mix. Put the remaining ice into a goblet and strain over the drink. Drink with a straw.
Serves 1, Preparation time: 3 minutes

Left to right: Sicilian Kiss; Tequila Sunrise

BEACHCOMBER

3 ice cubes, crushed
1 measure crème de menthe
soda water or lemonade
sprig of mint, to decorate

Put the ice into a wine goblet and pour the crème de menthe over.
Top up with soda water or lemonade. Decorate with the mint.
Serves 1, Preparation time: 3 minutes

BLUE MOON

5 ice cubes, cracked
¾ measure vodka
¾ measure Tequila
1 measure blue curaçao
lemonade

Put half the ice cubes into a mixing glass and add the vodka,
Tequila and blue curaçao. Stir to mix. Put the remaining ice into a
tall glass and strain over the cocktail. Top up with lemonade and
drink with a straw.
Serves 1, Preparation time: 3 minutes

Left to right: Blue Moon; Beachcomber

DRAMBUIE SHRUB

1 measure Drambuie
3 measures unsweetened orange juice, chilled
1 scoop lemon water ice
sprig of mint, to decorate

Pour the Drambuie into a goblet and add the orange juice. Stir together. Add the water ice, decorate with the mint and serve with straws and a spoon.

Serves 1, Preparation time: 3 minutes

GOLDEN LINING

3 ice cubes, cracked
1 measure Cointreau
1 measure Galliano
1 measure unsweetened orange juice
1 measure double cream
To decorate:
2 fresh cherries stalks joined or kumquats

Put the ice cubes into a cocktail shaker or screw-top jar and add the Cointreau, Galliano, orange juice and cream. Shake to mix. Strain into a tall glass and decorate the rim with the cherries and kumquats.

Serves 1, Preparation time: 5 minutes

ORANGE CLOUD

3 ice cubes, crushed
3 measures unsweetened orange juice
1 measure Pernod
To decorate:
1 slice orange
twist of orange peel

Put the ice into a tall glass and add the orange juice and Pernod. Stir well, add the slice of orange and peel, and serve with a stirrer.

Serves 1, Preparation time: 2 minutes

SHERRY COBBLER

3 ice cubes, crushed
2 slices orange
1 slice lemon
2 measures sherry
2 teaspoons sugar syrup
soda water

Put the ice into a champagne flute or tall glass. Cut each orange and lemon slice into 3 and put into the glass. Pour in the sherry and sugar syrup. Stir, then add a dash of soda water. Drink with a straw.

Serves 1, Preparation time: 4 minutes

Left to right: Golden Lining; Drambuie Shrub; Sherry Cobbler; Orange Cloud

CHAMPAGNE

Nothing induces the party spirit more quickly than champagne—those effervescent bubbles seem to convey a sense of occasion and magnify a mood—be it merely relaxing on a balmy evening, throwing an impromptu party or celebrating an important event. Champagne cocktails tend to be simple, enhancing the one taste rather than mingling many together. The finest and best known cocktails tend to marry the champagne with one other drink—orange juice, Guinness, brandy—to produce a sparkling combination. Purists may claim that at times nothing is better than a glass of champagne on its own, well chilled, but as a way of making a luxurious drink go a little further or even of making it a little more special, these champagne cocktails are hard to beat.

Champagne can only be made from grapes grown in a particular area in Northern France, and only according to strictly laid down, and enforced, methods. These are both lengthy and costly, hence the premium price. Less expensive and without the special finesse of the real thing but nevertheless very good are 'Methode Champenoise' sparkling wines. These are made by the same procedures as champagne but are produced in other areas, regions and countries. They are still superior to other sparkling wines and if champagne seems too extravagant you might like to use them instead.

The rules of mixing champagne cocktails are simple: always have the champagne well chilled, never attempt to use a blender, and mix it only at the last minute.

Secret Smile

PALM BEACH FIZZ

1 measure apricot brandy
1 measure unsweetened orange juice
¼ measure Grand Marnier
chilled champagne or sparkling dry white wine

Put the apricot brandy, orange juice and Grand Marnier into a champagne flute or cocktail glass and stir well. Carefully top up with the champagne or sparkling dry white wine.
Serves 1, Preparation time: 3 minutes

Variation:
Use peach brandy instead of apricot brandy and Galliano instead of Grand Marnier.

BLACK VELVET

1 part Guinness, chilled
1 part chilled champagne

Any size of glass can be used—300 ml/½ pint and 600 ml/1 pint goblets are particularly suitable—but remember when calculating amounts, the glass cannot be filled to the top as room has to be left for the 'head'. Pour some Guinness into a glass, then an equal amount of champagne.
Preparation time: 5 minutes

BUCK'S FIZZ

1 part fresh orange juice, chilled
1 part chilled champagne

Any size of glass can be used—a 300 ml/½ pint is a good size—but remember when calculating amounts, the glass cannot be filled to the top as room has to be left for the bubbling of the champagne. Buck's Fizz can also be made in a jug. Pour some orange juice into a chilled glass or a jug. Top up with an equal amount of champagne.
Preparation time: 5 minutes

KIR ROYALE

1 teaspoon Crème de Cassis
150-175 ml/5-6 fl oz chilled champagne or sparkling dry white wine

Measure the Crème de Cassis into a chilled tall glass or champagne flute. Pour in the champagne or sparkling wine and stir until just blended.
Serves 1, Preparation time: 5 minutes

Black Velvet; Kir Royale; Palm Beach Fizz

SECRET SMILE

lightly beaten egg white
caster sugar
1 measure unsweetened orange juice
½ measure Galliano
chilled champagne or sparkling dry white wine
twist of orange peel, to decorate

Dip the rim of a champagne flute or glass in the beaten egg white then caster sugar. Pour in the orange juice, then the Galliano, and top up with the champagne or sparkling wine. Decorate the rim of the glass with the orange slices.

Serves 1, Preparation time: 3 minutes

— CARIBBEAN CHAMPAGNE —

¼ measure light rum
¼ measure crème de banane
1 dash Angostura bitters
chilled champagne or sparkling dry white wine

To decorate:
1 slice banana
1 slice pineapple
cocktail cherries

Pour the rum, crème de banane and bitters into a champagne glass. Top with champagne and stir gently. Decorate with a slice of banana, pineapple and cherries speared with a cocktail stick.
Serves 1, Preparation time: 2 minutes

— CHAMPAGNE NORMANDE —

1 teaspoon Calvados
½ teaspoon sugar
1 dash Angostura bitters
chilled champagne or sparkling dry white wine
1 orange slice or orange peel spiral, to decorate

Put the Calvados, sugar and bitters in a champagne glass and stir until the sugar has dissolved. Top up with champagne, and decorate with orange slice or orange spiral.
Serves 1, Preparation time: 3 minutes

— BELLINI —

2 measures unsweetened peach juice (preferably fresh)
4 measures chilled champagne or sparkling dry white wine
1 dash grenadine (optional)

Mix the ingredients in a large wine glass.
Serves 1, Preparation time: 2 minutes

— BLUE CHAMPAGNE —

4 dashes blue curaçao
4 fl oz chilled champagne or sparkling dry white wine
1 slice orange, to decorate

Swirl the curaçao around the sides of a wine or champagne glass. Pour in the champagne and decorate with the orange slice.
Serves 1, Preparation time: 2 minutes

Blue Champagne; Caribbean Champagne; Champagne Normande

CLASSIC CHAMPAGNE COCKTAIL

1 sugar lump
1-2 drops Angostura bitters
1 measure brandy
4 measures chilled champagne
orange slice, to decorate

Put the sugar lump in a champagne glass and saturate with the Angostura bitters. Add the brandy and fill the glass with the champagne. Decorate with the orange slice.
Serves 1, Preparation time: 2 minutes

PERNOD FIZZ

1 measure Pernod
4 measures chilled champagne
1 slice of lime, to decorate

Put the Pernod into a champagne glass, and swirl it round. Slowly pour in the iced champagne allowing the drink to become cloudy. Decorate with lime.
Serves 1, Preparation time: 1 minute

Classic Champagne Cocktail; Chicago Cocktail; Pernod Fizz

CHICAGO COCKTAIL

lightly beaten egg white
caster sugar
3 ice cubes, crushed
dash Angostura bitters
dash curaçao
2 parts brandy
chilled champagne or sparkling dry white wine

Dip the rim of a glass in the egg white then sugar. Put the ice into a cocktail shaker or screw-top jar and add the bitters, curaçao and brandy. Shake and strain into the glass. Add the champagne.
Serves 1, Preparation time: 4 minutes

FRENCH '75

cracked ice
1 measure gin
juice of ½ lemon
1 teaspoon caster sugar
chilled champagne or sparkling dry white wine

Half fill a tall cocktail glass with cracked ice. Add the gin, lemon juice and sugar and stir well. Top up with chilled champagne.
Serves 1, Preparation time: 2 minutes

CUPS AND PUNCHES

Warm and welcoming or fresh and fruity, cups and punches are the perfect party drink. Offer mulled wine on a chilly night or summery Sangria at a garden party. Serving a cup or punch makes the host's job much easier than if he has to offer choices and remember requests. Since cups and punches are usually lighter on alcohol than individual drinks they are also a good but enjoyable way of regulating the intake at a party.

When choosing a wine to put in a cup, look out for the more fruity wines such as German or Alsatians, rieslings for white and any reds that are not too rough. All the receptacles such as bowl and glasses should be chilled before use. Any effervescent drinks such as sparkling wine or lemonade should be added at the last minute. This rule also applies to ice cubes (if they are used). Remember, though, that they will dilute a drink and it could be a better idea to place the cup/bowl in a larger one filled with ice.

Bowls for serving hot punches in must be heatproof. A hot punch will cool quickly if poured into a wide bowl so it is better to keep some back and keep it warm in a covered pan over low heat. Slow cookers can also be a useful way of keeping punches warm. When heating alcohol, if you wish to retain its alcoholic strength do not allow it to boil—just heat gently to below boiling point. When spices are used, add them to the covered punch for at least 15 minutes to allow the flavours to blend and try to use whole spices as they can be removed before serving and won't cloud the drink. Warm glasses before serving by immersing them in hot water.

Sherry Punch

TEA PUNCH

600 ml/1 pint China tea
100 g/4 oz sugar
juice of 2 lemons
juice of 1 orange
1 small vanilla pod
1 × 5 cm/2 inch cinnamon stick
150 ml/¼ pint brandy
150 ml/¼ pint dark rum
50 ml/2 fl oz Grand Marnier (optional)
about 300 ml/½ pint soda water, chilled
1 orange, sliced
1 lemon, sliced
Maraschino cherries

Leave the tea to infuse for 10 minutes, then strain into a saucepan. Add the sugar and heat gently until dissolved. Add the fruit juices, vanilla pod, cinnamon stick, brandy and rum, and heat gently to just below simmering for 5 minutes. Leave until cold, then chill for 2 hours. Remove the vanilla pod and cinnamon stick. Add the Grand Marnier, if using, and top up with soda water to taste. Float the fruit on top.

Makes about 8 glasses, Preparation time: 20 minutes, plus 10 minutes for infusing and 2 hours for chilling

ROSÉ CUP

ice cubes
1 × 70 cl/24.64 fl oz bottle sweet white wine, chilled
1 × 75 cl/26.40 fl oz bottle rosé wine, chilled
4 tablespoons Southern Comfort
450 ml/¾ pint tonic water, chilled
about 4 tablespoons canned mandarin segments

Put the ice in a chilled large bowl and pour the wines, Southern Comfort and tonic water over. Add the fruit and sufficient of their syrup to taste. Serve as soon as possible.

Makes 12-14 glasses, Preparation time: 5 minutes

SHERRY PUNCH

ice cubes
1 × 70 cl/24.64 fl oz bottle medium sherry, chilled
1 × 75 cl/26.40 fl oz bottle lemonade, chilled
50 ml/2 fl oz Mandarine Napoléon liqueur
cucumber slices
strawberries, whole and halved
1 orange, sliced

Put some ice cubes in a chilled large bowl and pour over the sherry, lemonade and liqueur, if using. Add the cucumber, fruit and mint. Serve as soon as possible.

Makes 12-13 glasses, Preparation time: 10 minutes

Left to right: Summer Cup; Rosé Cup

SUMMER CUP

1 × 70 cl/24.64 fl oz bottle Riesling, chilled
1 × 75 cl/26.40 fl oz bottle light red wine
75 ml/3 fl oz Drambuie
750 ml/1¼ pints lemonade, chilled
1 eating apple, sliced
1 orange, sliced
few fresh strawberries, halved
ice cubes

Pour the wines and Drambuie into a chilled large bowl. Add the lemonade, fruit and ice cubes. Serve as soon as possible.
Makes about 15 glasses, Preparation time: 5 minutes

WHITE WINE CUP

3 apricots or 1 peach, sliced (optional)
some fresh blackcurrants or strawberries
1 tablespoon caster sugar
75 ml/3 fl oz (or 1 miniature) Cointreau
1 × 70 cl/24.64 fl oz bottle medium dry white wine
1 × 70 cl/24.64 fl oz bottle Riesling

Put the fruit in a large bowl and sprinkle the sugar over. Chill for 30 minutes. Add the Cointreau and wine. Chill for 2 hours.

Makes 10-12 glasses, Preparation time: 10 minutes, plus 2½ hours for chilling

HONEYSUCKLE CUP

1 tablespoon clear honey
1 × 75 cl/26.40 fl oz bottle medium dry white wine
2 tablespoons Benedictine
150 ml/¼ pint brandy
750 ml/1¼ pints lemonade, chilled
1 peach, sliced
few fresh raspberries or strawberries

Put the honey in a large bowl and gradually stir in the wine. Add the Benedictine and brandy. Chill for 2 hours. Just before serving, add the lemonade and fruit.

Makes 10-12 glasses, Preparation time: 10 minutes, plus 2 hours for chilling

Left to right: White Wine Cup; Honeysuckle Cup

SANGRIA

ice cubes
2 × 75 cl/26.40 fl oz bottles Spanish red wine, chilled
120 ml/4 fl oz brandy (optional)
about 450 ml/¾ pint soda water, chilled
sliced seasonal fruit, e.g., apples, pears, oranges, lemons, peaches

Put some ice into a large bowl and pour over the wine and brandy, if using. Stir. Add soda water to taste and float the fruit on top.
Makes 11-12 glasses, Preparation time: 10 minutes

BOATMAN'S CUP

1 × 70 cl/24.64 fl oz bottle Riesling
500 ml/18 fl oz still dry cider
75 ml/3 fl oz brandy
about 175 ml/6 fl oz frozen orange juice concentrate, thawed
750 ml/1¼ pints lemonade, chilled
few black cherries, halved
1 slice orange
melon balls or cubes
sprigs of mint

Mix together the wine, cider, brandy and orange juice. Chill for 2 hours. Just before serving, add the lemonade, fruit and mint.
Makes 14-15 glasses, Preparation time: 10 minutes, plus 2 hours for chilling

Left to right: Sangria; Boatman's Cup

MULLED RED WINE

large pinch of ground ginger
1 tablespoon brown sugar
8 cloves
150 ml/¼ pint water
1 × 75 cl/26.40 fl oz bottle red wine
150 ml/¼ pint port

Mix the ginger with the sugar in a saucepan, then gently simmer with the cloves and water for 20 minutes. Strain. Gently heat with the wine for 5 minutes to just below simmering point. Add the port. Serve in warmed glasses or mugs.

Makes about 6 glasses or mugs, Preparation time: 35 minutes

MULLED MADEIRA

1 × 70 cl/24.64 fl oz bottle bual (sweet) Madeira
4 tablespoons brandy
4 tablespoons apricot brandy
300 ml/½ pint fresh orange juice
about 150 ml/¼ pint hot water
grated nutmeg

Gently heat the Madeira, brandies and orange juice in a saucepan to just below simmering point for 10 minutes. Add hot water to taste and serve in warmed glasses or mugs. Sprinkle nutmeg over the top.

Makes 10-12 glasses or mugs, Preparation time: 20 minutes

Left to right: Mulled Madeira; Mulled Red Wine

GLÜHWEIN

1 lemon
8 cloves
1 × 75 cl/26.40 fl oz bottle red wine
100 g/4 oz sugar
2 × 5 cm/2 inch cinnamon sticks
150 ml/¼ pint brandy

Spike the lemon with the cloves. Gently heat the wine, sugar, cinnamon sticks and lemon in a saucepan to just below simmering point for 10 minutes. Lower the heat and add the brandy. Warm for 2-3 minutes. Strain and serve immediately in warmed glasses or mugs.

Makes about 6 glasses or mugs, Preparation time: 20 minutes

GLÖGG

75 g/3 oz sugar
1 × 75 cl/26.40 fl oz bottle brandy
12 cloves
pinch of ground cinnamon
pinch of grated nutmeg
50 g/2 oz large raisins
50 g/2 oz unsalted blanched almonds
1 litre/1¾ pints medium sweet sherry

Gently dissolve the sugar in the brandy in a saucepan. Add the cloves, cinnamon, nutmeg, raisins and almonds, and heat to just below simmering point for 10 minutes. Heat the sherry separately to just below simmering point. Ignite the brandy mixture and pour in the sherry. Serve immediately in warmed glasses or mugs.

Makes 8-10 glasses or mugs, Preparation time: 20 minutes

Left to right: Glögg; Glühwein

RUM PUNCH

12 sugar lumps
2 oranges
2 lemons
1 litre/1¾ pints water
8 cloves
1 × 7.5 cm/3 inch cinnamon stick
600 ml/1 pint dark rum

Rub the sugar lumps over the rind of 1 orange and 1 lemon to remove the zest. Gently dissolve the sugar in the water in a saucepan. Add the cloves and cinnamon stick, and boil steadily for 5 minutes. Remove from the heat and add the rum. Cover and leave to infuse for 1 hour. Squeeze the orange and the lemon which have had the zest removed. Slice the remaining orange and lemon. Strain the punch, pour into a clean pan, and add the fruit juice. Reheat gently to just below simmering point. Float the remaining fruit on top and serve in warmed mugs or glasses.

Makes 9-10 mugs or glasses, Preparation time: 15 minutes, plus infusing

POLISH HONEY DRINK

about 6 tablespoons clear honey
300 ml/½ pint water
4 cloves
1 × 7.5 cm/3 inch cinnamon stick
1 vanilla pod
2 long strips lemon rind
2 long strips orange rind
1 × 75 cl/26.40 fl oz bottle vodka

Gently melt the honey in the water in a saucepan. Add the cloves, cinnamon stick, vanilla pod and fruit rinds, bring to the boil and simmer for 5 minutes. Cover, remove from the heat and leave to infuse for 1 hour. Strain and return to the cleaned pan. Add the vodka and gently heat to just below simmering point for 5 minutes. Serve in modest amounts in warmed glasses or mugs.

Makes about 8 glasses or mugs, Preparation time: 20 minutes, plus infusing

MULLED ALE (LAMB'S WOOL) –

6 cooking apples
36 cloves
large pinch of grated nutmeg
25 g/1 oz soft brown sugar
20 g/¾ oz unsalted butter
600 ml/1 pint sweet white wine
1 litre/1¾ pints strong ale

Spike the apples with the cloves. Place in a preheated oven and bake for about 40 minutes until very soft. Scoop out the flesh and beat in the nutmeg, sugar and butter. Gently heat the wine and ale in a saucepan to just below simmering point. Float the apple mixture on top. Ladle into warmed glasses or mugs and serve with spoons.

Makes 10-12 mugs, Preparation time: 10 minutes
Cooking time: about 40 minutes, Oven: 180°C, 350°F, Gas Mark 4

MULLED WHITE WINE

1 lemon
4 tablespoons clear honey
1 × 5 cm/2 inch cinnamon stick
1 × 70 cl/24.64 fl oz bottle medium dry white wine
4 tablespoons whisky
1 orange, sliced

Thinly pare the rind from the lemon and squeeze the juice. Mix the juice with the honey in a saucepan. Add the rind, cinnamon stick and wine, and heat gently to just below simmering point for 10 minutes. Remove the cinnamon stick. Add the whisky and sliced orange. Serve in warmed glasses or mugs.

Makes about 6 glasses or mugs, Preparation time: 15 minutes

Polish Honey Drink; Rum Punch

HOT TODDIES

Warming, cheering soothing, comforting—individual toddies can be made quickly, easily and simply and are excellent for providing personal central heating and cheering the spirit when cold and tired. What better pick-me-up than a nourishing Egg Nog? Or what better night cap than a Hot Toddy Supreme? While Irish Coffee provides the perfect luxurious end to a special meal. Before pouring a hot drink into a glass put a spoon into it to avoid cracking it and for easy handling use a glass with a metal holder or a mug with a handle.

For that 'morning-after' feeling you need a drink that packs a bit of a punch, to revive the jaded palate and recover drooping spirits. Fiery Tabasco, Worcestershire sauce and the Italian bitters 'Fernet Branca' are all traditional ingredients in these potent revivers. So if you do wake up feeling as if there's a cement mixer going round in your head, try one of these revivers.

Irish Coffee

BUTTERED RUM

50 ml/2 fl oz dark rum
1½ teaspoons soft brown sugar
200 ml/⅓ pint boiling water
15 g/½ oz unsalted butter
pinch of grated nutmeg

Measure the dark rum, sugar and 50 ml/2 fl oz of the water into a warmed cup, mug or glass. Add the butter and stir until melted. Add the remaining water and sprinkle the nutmeg over the top.

Serves 1, Preparation time: 5 minutes

EGG NOG

300 ml/½ pint milk
1 egg
1 tablespoon soft brown sugar
50 ml/2 fl oz Cognac
pinch of grated nutmeg

Heat the milk in a small saucepan to just below boiling point. Meanwhile, whisk the egg and sugar together in a small basin then whisk in the Cognac. Whisk in the hot milk then pour into a warmed mug, cup or glass. Sprinkle the nutmeg over the top.

Serves 1, Preparation time: 5 minutes

IRISH COFFEE

1 teaspoon sugar
1 measure Irish whiskey
about 150 ml/¼ pint hot, strong black coffee
1-2 tablespoons double cream

Put the sugar and whiskey into a warmed glass, pour in the coffee and stir until the sugar has dissolved. Pour the cream on to the surface over the back of a cold spoon.

Serves 1, Preparation time: 3 minutes

Variations:
Make as above substituting one of the following for the Irish whiskey.

Calypso coffee: Tia Maria
Caribbean coffee: rum
Royal or French coffee: cognac
German coffee: kirsch
Mexican coffee: Kahlua
Monks' coffee: Bénédictine or Chartreuse
Normandy coffee: Calvados
Prince Charles' coffee: Drambuie

Buttered Rum; Egg Nog

HOT TODDY SUPREME

2 measures Stone's Ginger Wine
1 measure brandy
1 tablespoon double cream
1 × 7.5 cm/3 inch cinnamon stick
½ teaspoon grated orange rind

Gently heat the Ginger Wine and brandy to just below boiling point.
Pour into a warmed cup or glass and gently pour the cream over the
back of a spoon on to the surface. Add the cinnamon stick and
sprinkle the orange rind over the surface.

Serves 1, Preparation time: 4 minutes

CAFÉ BRÛLOT

small strip of finely pared orange rind
1 × 2.5 cm/1 inch cinnamon stick
1 clove
1 teaspoon brown sugar
175 ml/6 fl oz strong black coffee
2 tablespoons Cognac

Put the orange rind, cinnamon stick, clover, sugar and coffee in a small saucepan and gradually bring to just below boiling point. Strain into a warmed coffee cup or glass. Warm the Cognac in a soup ladle, ignite and pour, flaming, into the coffee.

Serves 1, Preparation time: 5 minutes

SWEET DREAMS

250 ml/8 fl oz hot milk
70 ml/2½ fl oz Tia Maria
pinch of grated nutmeg

Pour the milk into a warmed cup or glass then stir in the Tia Maria. Sprinkle the nutmeg over the top.

Serves 1, Preparation time: 5 minutes

APPLE POSSET

200 ml/⅓ pint unswseetened apple juice
1 teaspoon soft brown sugar
2 tablespoons Calvados
1 × 5 cm/2 inch cinnamon stick

Heat the apple juice in a small saucepan to just below boiling point. Meanwhile, measure the sugar and Calvados into a warmed mug or glass. Pour the hot apple juice on to the Calvados, stirring with the cinnamon stick until the sugar has dissolved.

Serves 1, Preparation time: 5 minutes

TEA TODDY

1 measure Cointreau or curaçao
4 measures hot tea
slice of orange, to decorate

Pour the liqueur into a tall glass. Add hot tea, stir. Float the orange slice on top.

Serves 1, Preparation time: 1 minute

Café Brûlot; Sweet Dreams

HAIR OF THE DOG

3 ice cubes, crushed
½ measure Scotch whisky
1 measure double cream
½ measure clear honey

Put the ice cubes into a cocktail shaker or screw-top jar. Add the Scotch whisky, cream and honey and shake well to mix. Strain into a glass.

Serves 1, Preparation time: 3 minutes

PRAIRIE OYSTER

2 teaspoons tomato juice
1 egg yolk (unbroken)
2 dashes wine vinegar
pepper
1 teaspoon Worcestershire sauce
1 dash Tabasco sauce

Place all ingredients in a wine glass and stir carefully so as not to break the egg yolk; drink in one gulp.

Serves 1, Preparation time: 2 minutes

BLOODY MARY

1 measure vodka
2 measures tomato juice
dash of Worcestershire sauce
squeeze of lemon juice
cracked ice
celery salt, to taste
cayenne pepper, to taste
sprig of mint, to decorate

Place the vodka, tomato juice, Worcestershire sauce, lemon juice and cracked ice in a cocktail shaker or screw-topped jar. Shake to mix. Strain into a glass. Add celery salt and cayenne pepper to taste. Decorate with the mint.

Serves 1, Preparation time: 5 minutes

SUISSETTE

1 egg
2 ice cubes
1 measure Pernod

Break the egg into a glass and whisk with a fork. Add the ice cubes and pour in the Pernod. Stir and drink in one gulp.

Serves 1, Preparation time: 1 minute

Clockwise from top left: Bloody Mary; Hair of the Dog; Prairie Oyster

CAIPIRINHA

1 whole lime, quartered
1-2 teaspoons caster sugar
2 measures vodka
2 ice cubes, crushed

Place the quartered lime in an old-fashioned glass and add enough sugar to coat the fruit thoroughly. Mash the lime and the sugar together with a spoon and add the vodka and crushed ice.
Serves 1, Preparation time: 4 minutes

CORPSE REVIVER

2-3 ice cubes
1 measure brandy
½ measure Calvados
½ measure sweet vermouth

Put the ice into a cocktail shaker or screw-top jar and add the brandy, Calvados and vermouth. Shake to mix and strain into a cocktail glass.
Serves 1, Preparation time: 3 minutes

Corpse Reviver; Caipirinha

INDEX

INDEX